STEM SUPERWOMEN

Marie Curie

By Joseph Stanley

Cavendish Square

Published in 2026 by Cavendish Square Publishing, LLC
2544 Clinton Street Buffalo, NY 14224

Copyright © 2026 by Cavendish Square Publishing, LLC

No part of this publication may be reproduced, stored in a retrieval system, or transmitted in any form or by any means—electronic, mechanical, photocopying, recording, or otherwise—without the prior permission of the copyright owner. Request for permission should be addressed to Permissions, Cavendish Square Publishing, 2544 Clinton Street Buffalo, NY 14224. Tel (877) 980-4450; fax (877) 980-4454.

Website: cavendishsq.com

This publication represents the opinions and views of the author based on their personal experience, knowledge, and research. The information in this book serves as a general guide only. The author and publisher have used their best efforts in preparing this book and disclaim liability rising directly or indirectly from the use and application of this book.

All websites were available and accurate when this book was sent to press.

Library of Congress Cataloging-in-Publication Data

Names: Stanley, Joseph, author.
Title: Marie Curie / Joseph Stanley.
Description: First. | Buffalo, New York : Cavendish Square Publishing, [2026] | Series: The inside guide : STEM superwomen | Includes bibliographical references and index.
Identifiers: LCCN 2024059004 | ISBN 9781502674654 (library binding) | ISBN 9781502674647 (paperback) | ISBN 9781502674661 (ebook)
Subjects: LCSH: Curie, Marie, 1867-1934–Juvenile literature. | Women physicists–Poland–Biography–Juvenile literature. | Women physicists–France–Biography–Juvenile literature. | Women chemists–Poland–Biography–Juvenile literature. | Women chemists–France–Biography–Juvenile literature. | Nobel Prize winners–Biography–Juvenile literature.
Classification: LCC QD22.C8 S73 2026 | DDC 540.92 [B]–dc23/eng/20250101
LC record available at https://lccn.loc.gov/2024059004

Editor: Katie Kawa
Designer: Deanna Lepovich

The photographs in this book are used by permission and through the courtesy of: Cover, pp. 15 (top), 21, 28 (bottom left) Everett Collection/Shutterstock.com; p. 4 Eva Pruchova/Shutterstock.com; p. 6 marekusz/Shutterstock.com; p. 8 (main) Plac Zamkowy z namiotami wojska rosyjskiego (1861)/Wikimedia Commons; p. 8 (inset) Sklodowski Family Wladyslaw and his daughters Maria Bronislawa Helena/Wikimedia Commons; p. 9 Maria Sklodowska et sa soeur Bronislawa en 1886/Wikimedia Commons; p. 10 Marie and Pierre Curie Converse/Wikimedia Commons; p. 12 Tatiana Diuvbanova/Shutterstock.com; p. 13 OSweetNature/Shutterstock.com; p. 14 Panggabean/Shutterstock.com; p. 15 (bottom) Bjoern Wylezich/Shutterstock.com; p. 16 Pierre Curie et Marie Sklodowska Curie 1895/Wikimedia Commons; p. 18 Marie Curie 1903/Wikimedia Commons; p. 19 Marie Pierre Irene Curie/Wikimedia Commons; pp. 20, 29 (right) Mark_Kostich/Shutterstock.com; p. 22 courtesy of the Library of Congress; p. 24 Roman Belogorodov/Shutterstock.com; p. 25 EQRoy/Shutterstock.com; p. 26 Irène, Marie et Ève Curie/Wikimedia Commons; p. 27 SpeedKingz/Shutterstock.com; p. 28 (top left) Francisco Javier Diaz/Shutterstock.com; p. 28 (top right) Wright First Flight 1903Dec17 (full restore 115)/Wikimedia Commons; p. 28 (bottom right) meunierd/Shutterstock.com; p. 29 (left) Morphart Creation/Shutterstock.com.

Some of the images in this book illustrate individuals who are models. The depictions do not imply actual situations or events.

CPSIA compliance information: Batch #CSCSQ26: For further information contact Cavendish Square Publishing LLC at 1-877-980-4450.

Printed in the United States of America

Find us on

CONTENTS

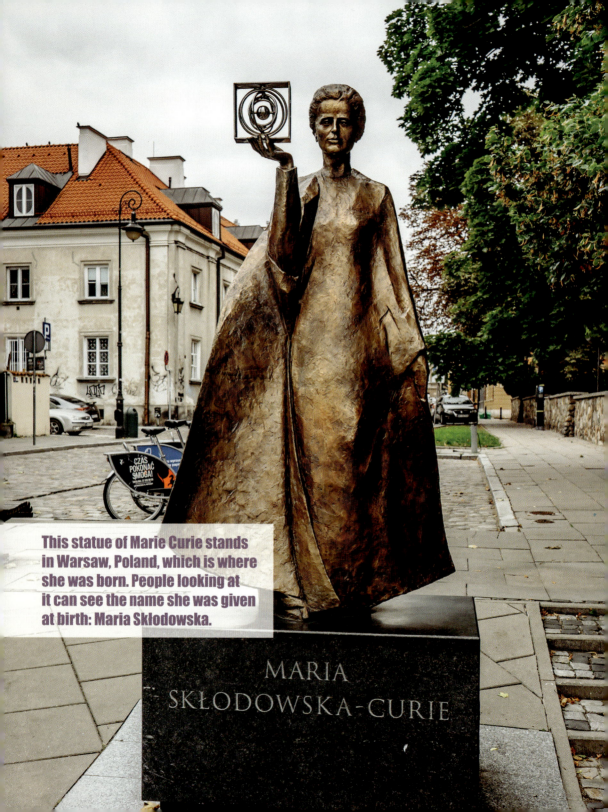

This statue of Marie Curie stands in Warsaw, Poland, which is where she was born. People looking at it can see the name she was given at birth: Maria Skłodowska.

MARIA
SKŁODOWSKA-CURIE

Many people around the world know the story of Marie Curie's work with radioactive materials. The discoveries she made while working in France changed many fields of science, including chemistry and medicine, forever.

However, Marie's story didn't begin with her work in France. Instead, it began many years before in what's now the country of Poland. Back then, Marie was known as Maria, and she wasn't a famous scientist. She was just a young girl who loved to learn.

Proud to Be Polish

Maria Skłodowska was born on November 7, 1867, in the city of Warsaw, which is now the capital of the nation of Poland. When Maria was born, however, Warsaw was controlled by the Russian Empire. Poland been under the rule of different empires for a long time, but many of its people continued to hold on to their Polish identity.

Fast Fact

Radioactive materials emit energy when the atoms they're made of decay, or break down over time. They do this spontaneously—all on their own.

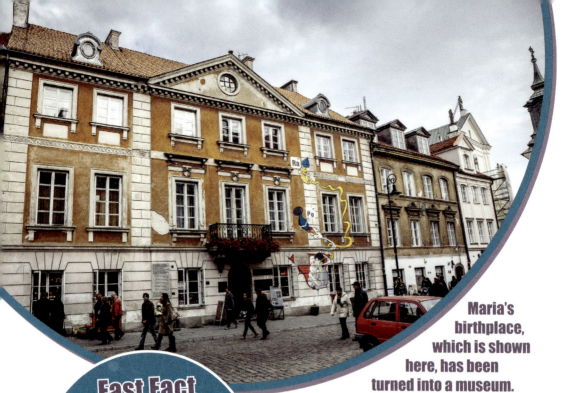

Maria's birthplace, which is shown here, has been turned into a museum.

Fast Fact

Maria's mother, Bronisława, was the head of a boarding school for girls. However, she quit her job when Maria was born to focus on raising her family.

Maria's parents were two such Polish people. They were teachers with a strong family history of resistance to the rule of other empires. Maria's father, Władysław, eventually lost his job because of this.

Loss and Learning

After Maria's father lost his job, things continued to go wrong for the Skłodowska family. When Maria was seven years old, her oldest sister, Zofia, died of a sickness called typhus. Just three years later, Maria's mother died of a different sickness—tuberculosis.

Maria and her three remaining siblings—her older sisters Bronisława and Helena and her older brother Józef—had only their father, and

CONGRESS POLAND

Maria was born in what's known as Congress Poland, or the Congress Kingdom of Poland. It got its name from the Congress of Vienna, which ended the Napoleonic Wars. These were wars fought from around 1800 to 1815 between France, which was under the rule of Napoleon Bonaparte, and other European powers. When the wars ended, parts of Europe, including Poland, were divided between those powers.

Congress Poland was ruled by the czar, or leader, of Russia. Poland was supposed to have some autonomy, or independence, but the czar's rule was **strict**. Many Polish people fought back against foreign rule until Poland gained independence after World War I (1914-1918).

Władysław did the best he could. Because he could no longer teach students in a laboratory, he brought his lab equipment home and used it to teach his children about science.

Fast Fact

Under Russian rule, Polish students weren't allowed to use laboratory equipment in school.

A Secret School

Maria did well in school. Years later, she recalled always being at the top of her class. However, after she graduated, she struggled with her mental health. Spending some time in the countryside with relatives who lived there helped her, and she came back to the city ready to learn more.

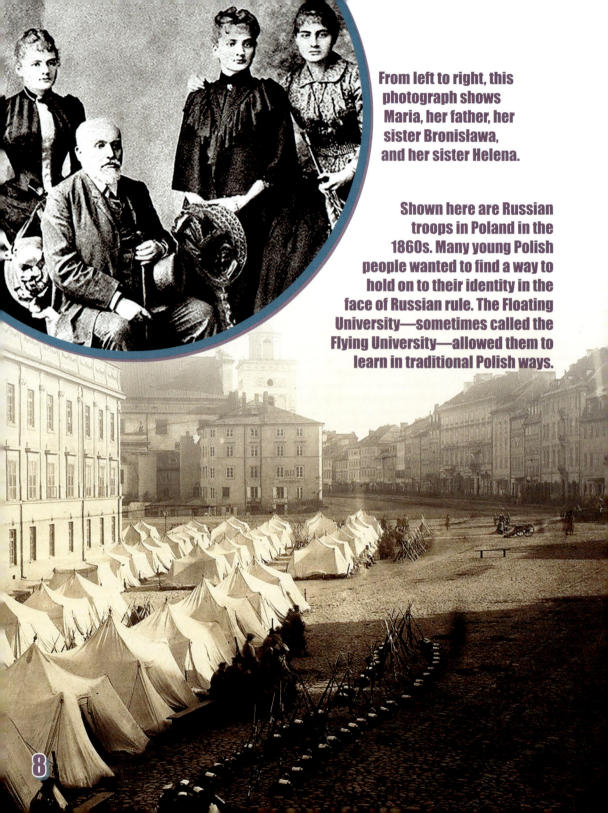

From left to right, this photograph shows Maria, her father, her sister Bronisława, and her sister Helena.

Shown here are Russian troops in Poland in the 1860s. Many young Polish people wanted to find a way to hold on to their identity in the face of Russian rule. The Floating University—sometimes called the Flying University—allowed them to learn in traditional Polish ways.

There was a big problem, though. Women couldn't go to college at the University of Warsaw. Maria and Bronisława didn't let that stop them. They joined what's known as the Floating University, which held classes in secret. It got its name from the fact that classes "floated" from place to place so students wouldn't get caught.

A Promise Between Sisters

If Maria and Bronisława wanted to get a formal university education, they needed to leave Poland, but they didn't have enough money to do this. However, they came up with a plan. Maria would stay in Poland and work to pay for Bronisława's education in Paris, France. Then, when Bronisława finished school, she would pay for Maria's education in Paris.

While Maria worked and waited her turn, she continued to study. She read books about chemistry, **physics**, and math. She even worked in a laboratory. She knew she wanted to study science and math in Paris.

Maria (*left*) and Bronisława (*right*) both became scientists. Bronisława became a medical doctor.

Paris is where Maria met Pierre Curie, who became her husband. They are shown together in this photograph.

Chapter Two

ELEMENTAL DISCOVERIES

In 1891, it was finally Maria's turn to study in Paris. Moving to France changed her life in many ways. It even changed her name! She was no longer Maria; she was Marie. Eventually, her last name would change, too, but first, she needed to do what she'd come to Paris for—study science and math.

Studying at the Sorbonne

When Marie arrived in France, she began attending classes at the University of Paris, which is also known as the Sorbonne. At first, she lived with her sister and her new brother-in-law, but she soon moved into her own space. Life wasn't always easy for Marie. She didn't have a lot of money, but she was willing to struggle if it meant she could get a university degree.

Marie ended up getting a degree—and another one! In 1893, she received a degree in physics, and in 1894, she got one in math.

Fast Fact

Before traveling to France, Marie earned money by working as a governess. A governess is a woman who takes care of children in a private home.

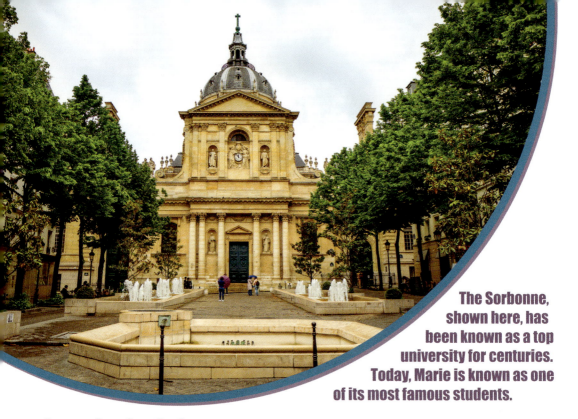

The Sorbonne, shown here, has been known as a top university for centuries. Today, Marie is known as one of its most famous students.

Love in the Laboratory

Marie's life in Paris included conducting experiments to study how well different kinds of steel could work as magnets. However, it wasn't easy for her to find a laboratory to work in. Her search for a laboratory led to a meeting with Pierre Curie, who was well known for his research on magnets.

Marie and Pierre enjoyed each other's company and respected each other as scientists. Soon, this grew into love. They got married in 1895 and became a true "power couple" whose work together changed science forever.

Fast Fact

Marie went back to Poland after getting her math degree in 1894. However, Pierre convinced her to come back to France to continue her work—and their relationship.

12

Researching Radioactivity

Marie became very interested in Henri Becquerel's work with an element called uranium. In 1896, he discovered that uranium emitted rays, now known as radiation, that acted like weaker versions of the X-rays that had been discovered the year before.

Marie tested the air around uranium samples and discovered that Henri was right—uranium does give off its own rays. She also discovered those rays stayed the same no matter what was done to the uranium. This meant radiation came from the uranium atom. This was a new discovery that changed how we think about atoms!

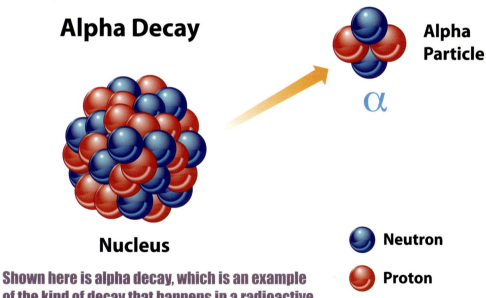

Alpha Decay

Alpha Particle

α

Nucleus

Neutron

Proton

Shown here is alpha decay, which is an example of the kind of decay that happens in a radioactive element. In this kind of decay, protons and neutrons are emitted.

New Elements

Marie had been working mainly with uranium, which is its own element. An element is matter that is made up of only one kind of atom. She found uranium in different minerals, including one called pitchblende.

WHY DID IT MATTER?

What was so special about Marie's understanding of radioactivity? By figuring out that an atom can be radioactive, Marie helped scientists draw closer to understanding that atoms aren't the smallest things to exist in the universe. In fact, they're made up of smaller particles, which are emitted by radioactive elements.

Protons, which have a positive charge, and neutrons, which don't have a charge, make up the nucleus, or center, of an atom. Electrons, which have a negative charge, circle around the nucleus. Marie's work with radioactivity helped other scientists see that atoms can be divided into these smaller parts. This led to the understanding of atoms that we have today.

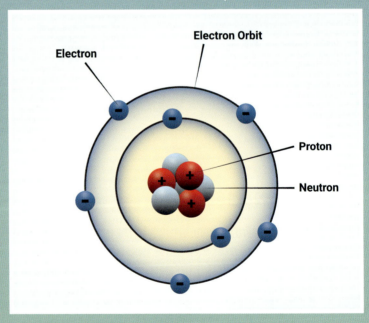

For a long time, scientists believed an atom couldn't be broken down into smaller parts (*shown here*). Marie's work helped to change that belief because radiation came from atoms breaking down.

Fast Fact

It's believed that Marie was the first person to use the word "radioactivity."

Marie and Pierre achieved something most scientists can only dream of— discovering a new element—and they did it twice!

Marie soon discovered that pitchblende is more radioactive than pure uranium. This made her wonder if it contained another radioactive element.

Pierre stopped his studies to help Marie analyze, or closely look at, pitchblende. By separating different parts and testing those parts for radioactivity, they found two new elements in 1898. Polonium was named after Marie's home country, and radium was named after the Latin word for "ray."

This rock contains pitchblende.

Marie and Pierre Curie were partners in science and in life. However, that partnership was tragically cut short in 1906.

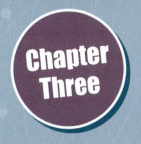
HIGHS AND LOWS

The first years of the 20th century were a happy time for Marie and Pierre Curie. Their work with radioactivity and their discovery of polonium and radium led to scientific success and worldwide fame.

Their happiness wouldn't last long, though. The highs soon gave way to painful lows that left Marie alone in her work—and her life.

The Nobel Prize

Marie and Pierre's work with radioactive elements earned them a lot of attention and respect. However, that respect wasn't always given to Marie. Even though she was the one who started their experiments with radioactivity, some of her fellow scientists ignored her **contributions** simply because she was a woman.

Fast Fact

Marie and Pierre had two daughters. Irène was born in 1897, and Ève was born in 1904.

For example, in 1903, Marie joined Pierre and Henri in receiving the Nobel Prize in Physics for their work with radioactivity. This almost didn't happen, though. The scientists who gave out the prize only wanted to give it to Pierre and Henri. When Pierre

Fast Fact

The Nobel Prize is given to the people who have made the biggest positive impact on humanity each year. Nobel Prizes are given out in five different areas: physics, chemistry, medicine, literature, and peace. There is also a related prize given for economics.

Shown here is a photograph of Marie taken to honor her Nobel Prize in 1903. Winners of the prize receive money, and Marie and Pierre used their money to continue their research.

learned of this, he complained, and Marie was then included. She became the first woman to win a Nobel Prize.

A Terrible Loss

Marie and Pierre continued to work together, and Pierre was given an offer to become a professor at the Sorbonne. Tragedy struck, however, when Pierre was killed while crossing the street in Paris on April 19, 1906. He was hit by a wagon being pulled by horses, leaving Marie to continue their work on her own.

Pierre's death was difficult for the whole Curie family. Marie was the only one left to make a living to support her family.

One of the ways Marie continued their work was by taking over Pierre's teaching position at the Sorbonne. She became a professor of physics, making her the first female professor in the history of the Sorbonne.

Fast Fact

Marie earned her doctorate—the most advanced degree a person can get—from the Sorbonne in 1903.

A Second Nobel Prize

Marie remained hard at work, and she came up with a standard unit that could be used to measure radiation. Today, it's known as the curie—named for its creator. Marie's scientific discoveries reached far beyond her laboratory too. Not long after she discovered radium, doctors began using it to treat cancer. In addition, scientists started using radiation to help them figure out the age of Earth.

Because of the importance of Marie's work, she was awarded a Nobel Prize in Chemistry in 1911. This made her the first person to win two Nobel Prizes.

A Woman at War

In 1914, World War I broke out, and France was the site of many of the war's battles. Marie believed science could help the soldiers, so

TREATING CANCER WITH RADIATION

Pierre Curie discovered that radiation could harm the body's tissues, or the groups of cells that make up body parts. Marie and Pierre believed this meant that radiation could be used to treat cancer, which is a sickness that causes cells to grow in ways they shouldn't.

The Curies were correct, and today, radiation is a common treatment for many kinds of cancer. In one kind of treatment, the radiation comes from outside the patient's body. In another kind of treatment, the source of the radiation is placed inside the body, near the area affected by cancer. This kind of treatment is sometimes called curietherapy.

Today, when people are treated for cancer with radiation, they sometimes have to wear a special mask to keep their head still during treatment. This makes sure the rays go where they need to.

she once again got to work. She developed traveling X-ray machines that could be sent to battlefields to help the doctors there. These machines could help doctors find broken bones, bullets, and other dangers in the body that couldn't be seen before.

Before the year was over, Marie and her daughter Irène traveled into a war zone for the first time to bring this technology to the troops.

Many wounded soldiers were helped using Marie's mobile X-ray units during World War I, which ended in 1918. Marie taught other women how to use the machines so they could play a part in the war effort too.

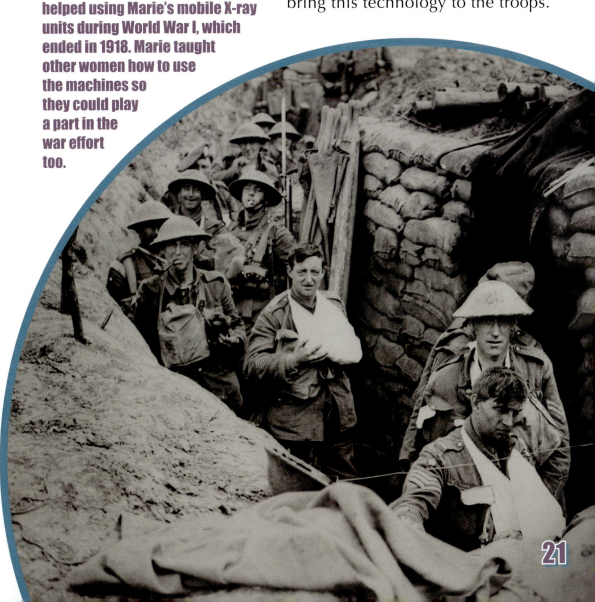

Marie was exposed to high levels of radiation for many years because of her work. This kind of exposure can lead to serious health problems.

LIVING AND DYING FOR HER WORK

After World War I, Marie focused on running the Radium Institute. This was a laboratory and research center that would focus on studying radiation, especially its use in medicine.

Radiation can help people with cancer get healthy, but today we know it can also cause people to get sick if they're exposed to too much of it. At the time, Marie didn't fully know the dangers of her work, but it would eventually catch up with her.

A Surprising Sickness

Radioactivity was such a new discovery that no one knew yet what it would do to a person's body over time. Marie continued to work, but the effects of that work on her body began to show. She had vision problems and sometimes felt too sick to go to her laboratory.

Marie died on July 4, 1934. It's believed that she had a kind of anemia, which is a condition

Fast Fact

In 1921, Marie visited the United States. A group of Americans, including many women, had raised money to give Marie radium to take back to France to continue her research.

in which the body doesn't have enough blood cells to function. Blood cells are made in **bone marrow**, which can be damaged by long-term exposure to radiation.

Fast Fact

Marie's papers are considered so radioactive that they have to be kept away from people in a special box. Anyone who wants to handle them must wear protective clothing!

The Curie Institute

Before Marie died, she set up the Curie Foundation. Its goal was to

Marie is buried with other famous French people in a building known as the Panthéon. Marie was the first woman buried there because of her own accomplishments. Pierre is buried there as well.

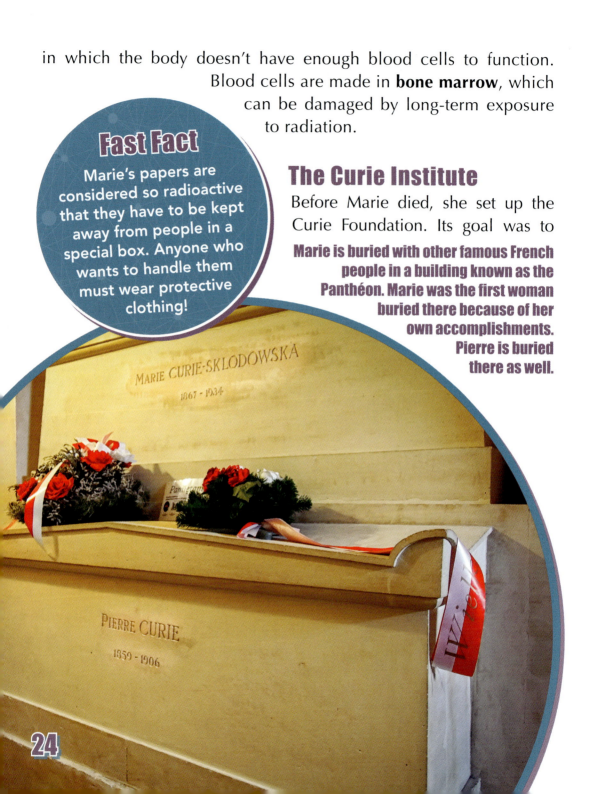

MARIE CURIE-SKLODOWSKA

1867 - 1934

PIERRE CURIE

1859 - 1906

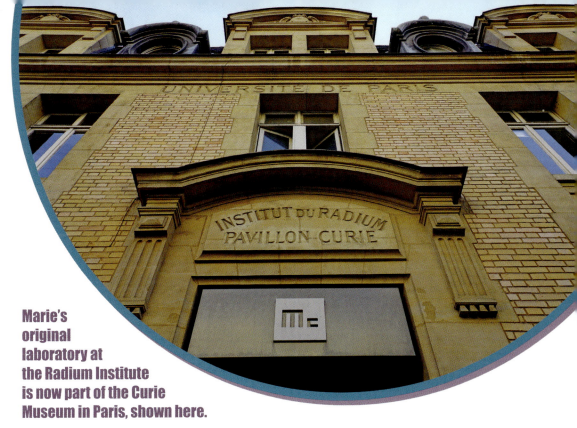

Marie's original laboratory at the Radium Institute is now part of the Curie Museum in Paris, shown here.

raise money to support the work being done at the Radium Institute. Marie knew the Radium Institute would be an important part of her **legacy**, and that is still true today.

Now known as the Curie Institute (or Institut Curie in French), it is the leading cancer research and treatment center in France and one of the top cancer centers in the world. At the Institute, doctors and other scientists continue Marie's work by discovering the latest advances in science and technology that can be used to treat cancer.

The Family Business

The Curie scientific legacy didn't end with Marie. Irène also became a famous scientist. She worked closely with her husband, Frédéric Joliot-Curie. In fact, they met while working at the Radium Institute.

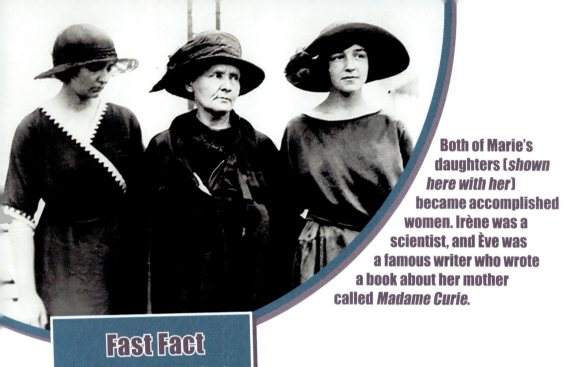

Both of Marie's daughters (*shown here with her*) became accomplished women. Irène was a scientist, and Ève was a famous writer who wrote a book about her mother called *Madame Curie*.

Fast Fact

As of 2025, the Curie family holds the record for most Nobel Prizes won by a single family.

In 1935, they won the Nobel Prize in Chemistry for their work with **artificial** radiation.

Another member of Marie's family won a Nobel Prize in 1965. That year, Ève's husband, Henry Richardson Labouisse, accepted the Nobel Peace Prize won by the children's organization UNICEF. He was the director of UNICEF at the time.

Changing the World

Marie Curie's interest in STEM—science, technology, engineering, and math—took her from secret schools in Poland to her own laboratory in Paris and multiple Nobel Prizes. She often had to fight to be taken seriously as a woman in STEM, but her work spoke for itself.

Today, Marie continues to inspire women to turn their interest in STEM into a career. From women working in cancer hospitals to

GETTING GIRLS INVOLVED

Marie encouraged women to get involved in science—whether it was by teaching them how to operate mobile X-ray units or giving them jobs in her laboratory. Today, many different groups are working to continue that encouragement by supporting women and girls in STEM. For example, the National Girls Collaborative Project works with different organizations across the United States to support STEM programs for girls.

Marie once said, "Nothing in life is to be feared; it is only to be understood." Groups that support girls in STEM know that increasing their understanding can help them feel empowered, **confident**, and brave.

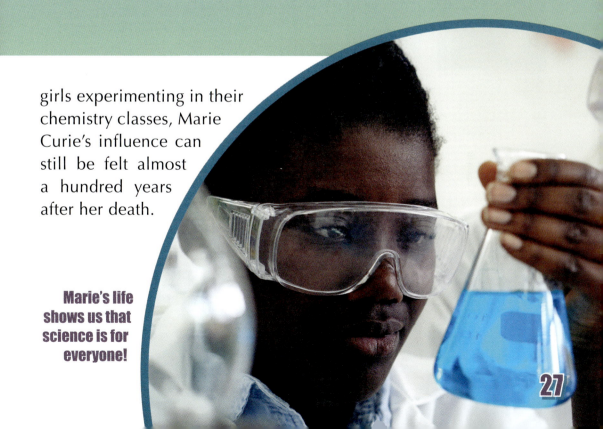

girls experimenting in their chemistry classes, Marie Curie's influence can still be felt almost a hundred years after her death.

Marie's life shows us that science is for everyone!

TIMELINE

In Marie's Life	World Events

1861-1865
The American Civil War is fought.

1867
Maria Skłodowska is born on November 7 in Poland.

1891
Maria moves to Paris to study and becomes known as Marie.

1903
Marie wins her first Nobel Prize for her work with radioactivity.

1903
Orville and Wilbur Wright fly an airplane for the first time.

1908
The Ford Model T is introduced and becomes the first car that average Americans can afford.

1911
Marie wins her second Nobel Prize for the discovery of polonium and radium.

1914-1918
World War I is fought.

1929
The Great Depression begins.

1934
Marie dies on July 4.

1. Why do you think women in Marie's time weren't allowed to go to college in Poland?

2. What do you think was Marie's greatest discovery, and why?

3. What are some ways Marie's discoveries are still helping us today?

4. When Marie said, "Nothing in life is to be feared; it is only to be understood," what do you think she meant? Do you agree?

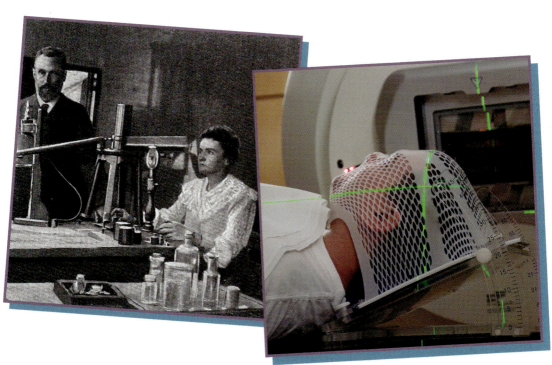

GLOSSARY

artificial: Made by people and not by nature.

bone marrow: Soft tissue that is inside a body's bones and is where blood cells are made.

confident: Having a feeling of belief that you can do something well.

contribution: Something that plays a big part in making something else happen.

emit: To throw or give off or out.

legacy: The lasting effect of a person or thing.

physics: The branch of science that deals with matter and energy, as well as how they interact.

relationship: A pairing of people joined by feelings of love.

strict: Relating to a rule or law that is very narrow in its view and does not allow for flexibility.

tragically: Very sadly.

FIND OUT MORE

Books

Howell, Izzi. *Marie Curie*. Denver, CO: Peterson's Publishing, 2020.

MacCarald, Clara. *Marie Curie: Radiation Pioneer*. Minneapolis, MN: Jump!, 2024.

Marshall, Linda Elovitz. *Sisters in Science: Marie Curie, Bronia Dluska, and the Atomic Power of Sisterhood*. New York, NY: Alfred A. Knopf, 2023.

Websites

Marie Curie and the Science of Radioactivity
history.aip.org/exhibits/curie/
The American Institute of Physics presents a very detailed biography of Marie Curie, featuring many quotes from the scientist.

National Geography Kids: Marie Curie
kids.nationalgeographic.com/history/article/marie-curie
National Geographic kids provides readers with a look at Marie Curie's life, including historical photographs.

The Nobel Prize
www.nobelprize.org
This official website provides information about the Nobel Prize, such as biographies of past winners, including Marie and Pierre Curie.

Publisher's note to educators and parents: Our editors have carefully reviewed these websites to ensure that they are suitable for students. Many websites change frequently, however, and we cannot guarantee that a site's future contents will continue to meet our high standards of quality and educational value. Be advised that students should be closely supervised whenever they access the internet.

INDEX